INSTAGRAM SECRETS (VOL.6)

How to use Instagram METRICS

Become an influencer and build a business with no money

Short social media marketing book

By Rossitza Toneva

Table of content

Why should you read this book?

"Marketing without data and analytics is like driving with your eyes closed." **Dan Zarrella**

Instagram Insights can help you build a social strategy based on real data.

Insights data can help you better understand your customers.
What do they like?
When do they spend most of their time online?
How can you better reach them?
These are some of the critical questions you need to answer when you're trying to market your product or service.

The more data and answers you have, the more tailored you can be in your marketing approach, and the more likely you are to share content that engages with your followers.

While there are many analytics tools available for Instagram, Instagram Insights is a free tool, and you can use it without leaving the app.

It's a great place to start if you're interested in finding out more about your followers.

Instagram Insights can help make better decisions based on data, not just feelings. This Instagram tool is fundamental to set up an efficient social strategy.

This book can help you to understand better the Instagram Insight languages.

To determine the level of success that you achieve, you must be able to measure your progress. When you measure your progress, you can see how you're coming along, and this is a powerful motivator to help you stick with it. The fact that you know you are making good progress gives you a realistic picture of the situation.

How can I get money with my Instagram profile?

"The best way to predict your future is to create it." **Abraham Lincoln**

You have in your hands the first volume of twelve pieces puzzle named "Instagram Secrets." This puzzle includes the following pieces:

HOW to find the right Instagram AUDIENCE?
HOW to Build the Perfect Instagram PROFILE?
HOW to create Instagram KILLER CONTENTS?
HOW to outsmart Instagram ALGORITHM?
HOW to use Instagram HASHTAGS?
HOW to use Instagram METRICS?
HOW to use Instagram DIRECT MESSAGING?
HOW to use Instagram IGTV content?
HOW to use Instagram CONTESTS?
HOW to use Instagram INFLUENCERS?
HOW to use Instagram AUTOMATION TOOLS?
How to generate PROFITS from Instagram?

Each element above contributes to growing your Instagram account. You have to understand the secrets of all twelve pieces. That's why I created a set of 12 books. Thanks to this step- by –step set of books, you are going to learn a lot of tricks that nobody shares with you.

Instagram is the leading social media platform, with over a billion monthly users, 71% under 35. So if you want to build a business and your target is millennials, Instagram is the right communication platform.

Keep in mind that there are three significant ways to make money on Instagram.

- Work as an influencer to post content sponsored by brands.
- Be an affiliate marketer selling other people's products.
- Become or be an entrepreneur and sell your products or service.

You can learn more about these specific topics in the last book of the collection: Instagram Secrets Vol 12: How to generate PROFITS from Instagram. Become an influencer and build a business with no money on Instagram.

So keep reading all twelve books.

You can find the entire books collection on the next pages:

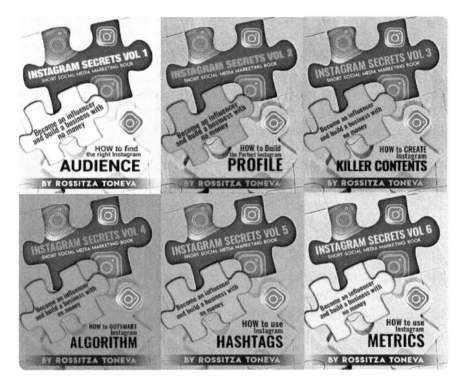

These are the first six books of the collection. Thanks to these first books, you will learn the essential Instagram tools: AUDIENCE; PROFILE; KILLER CONTENTS ALGORITHM; HASHTAGS; METRICS.

The next image contains the other six books: DIRECT MESSAGING; IGTV CONTENT; CONTEST; INFLUENCERS; AUTOMATION TOOLS; PROFITS.

So once you read through this set of 12 books, I am convinced you are going to become a real Instagram expert. Make sure that you read and understand each book before you move to the next one. You will quickly see that all book strategies are connected. Only when you get the whole picture, you can fully understand how to create your Winning Instagram strategy.

Think that thanks to Instagram, you could turn your passions into money and build a business, but before, you must know all the Powerful Secrets.

Growing your Instagram following requires consistent commitment and dedication. You will not get the results you are looking for if you are not working and build your Instagram page every single day. So you need to think about:

What are you looking to get out of Instagram?

Why are you making an Instagram account?

What kind of goals do you want to achieve with your Instagram account: follower growth, brand awareness, or just revenue?

All my short step by step guides have a section named Homework task. So take your time to write down your ideas. I am going to help you to clarify your thoughts, guiding you step by step.

The homework section is critical because it offers you the opportunity to understand what to do in this first stage. Try to experiment with all the ideas you write down in the Homework section using your Instagram profile. When you write down your thoughts, you automatically focus your full attention on them. Remember that you have to experiment.

Before we start, I would like to give you a special bonus - the opportunity to get one of my books for FREE. Send me an email at rtineva8o@gmail.com. Please indicate the name of the book that you bought and the day. Send the name of the new book as well.

You can contact me for a personal Skype session as well.

Please do not forget if you enjoyed this book and found some benefit in reading it, to post an Amazon review. Your feedback and support will help me to improve my writing craft for future projects significantly. And make this book even better.

In this specific short guide, I'll teach you the importance of measuring your Instagram performance.

Introduction

One of the most important things before you start an activity is to set up your goals and to track your progress.

Social media has become an essential tool because you can track all your campaigns. That's why these instruments are fundamental today. Each social media network has its own-app tools available to track metrics within the app. By monitoring these stats, you will know if what you are doing on social media is helping you achieve your goals.

One of the significant innovations of Instagram has been **'Insights.'** This tool allowing users to view analytics measuring the performance of their content and better understand their target audience. These figures will show you what works and what doesn't. Without all these data, you're completely blind. With it, you're on the road to get 5.000 or 10.000 followers.

Always think that the first step to measuring your performance depends on your goal-setting stage. You must set a goal that can be measured easly. Take a moment to evaluate what you want to do with your Instagram account and start setting goals to achieve it.

Goals will give you direction.

Specific goals for your Instagram account could be:

Increase engagement rate

Increasing product/ service sales, using Instagram

Increase my followers

Driving traffic to your website or YouTube channel

Identifying and establishing relationships with influencers

Increasing brand awareness

So, before you start any Instagram activity, I will teach you where to find all data to track your performance.

Chapter 1: What are Instagram Insights and how to use them?

Instagram Insights is the data collection and analytics tool. This data instrument tracks who follows you, what they like or comment on, your reach and impressions, and much more. With Instagram Insights, you can learn more about your target audience and how they engage with the content you post on your Account.

This information is critical to set up a successful Instagram strategy because each Account is unique. What works for one Profile won't necessarily work for all profiles.

The Main aim of Instagram Insights is to help you learn more about your followers. And what kind of users interact with your brand on Instagram. The information provided are details about the age, gender, and location of the people who follow you. You also have access to information about which stories and feeds are engaged with the most.

How to access Instagram Insights

Accessing Instagram Insights is relatively fast and straightforward. There is one crucial thing you'll need to take first. If you don't already have a business account, you'll need to convert your Account.

If you already have a business account, skip the next section.

How to convert to an Instagram business account

To convert your current private Profile to a business Instagram account, start by logging in, then follow the steps below.

Step 1: Tap the hamburger icon in the top-right corner of your Profile.

Step 2: Tap the gear icon for "Settings."

Step 3: Next, hit "Account."

Step 4: Then hit "Switch to Business Profile."

Step 5: Connect to your business Facebook Profile if you have one, and add additional business details as directed by Instagram.

Step 6: Tap "Done."

Check the pictures below.

Steps 1 and 2.

Steps 3 and 4

After you switched your Account in Bussiness account, you can find the Insight section following the steps below:

Step 1: Tap the hamburger icon in the top-right corner of your Profile.

Step 2: Tap the gear icon for "Insights."

You can see the image on the next page for further details

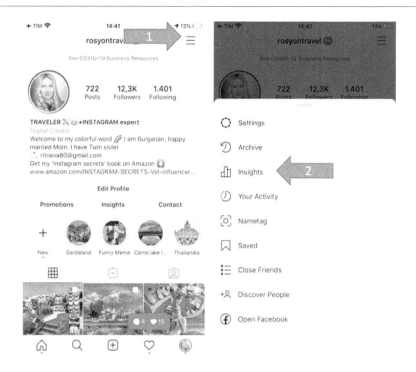

Instagram Insights is splited into the following three categories, each category containing different information:

• ACCOUNTS REACHED (ACTIVITY for the old Insight version of Instagram)

• CONTENT INTERACTIONS (CONTENT for the old Insight versione of Instagram)

• TOTAL FOLLOWERS (AUDIENCE for the old Insight version)

In the next chapters, we'll dive into how you can use all that data to set up a successful Instagram marketing strategy.

The insight section provides a view of account performance over the last seven days. Note that these seven days don't include the day when you are checking your insights. To give you an example, if you check your Insights on Tuesday, you will find all data from Monday to Monday.

Chapter 2: Accounts reached analytics

The first Insight section is named **Accounts reached** or Account Activity. Tap on this section to open all sub- sections illustrated in the next pages.

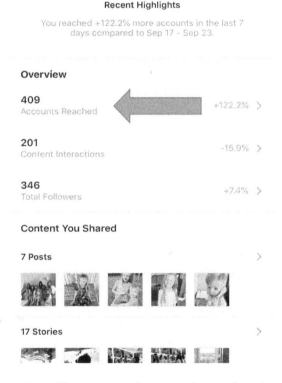

This first section illustrates the number of unique accounts that have seen any of your posts, storirs, or IGTV videos. This section is limited to the past seven days.

The **Accounts Reached** section has the following subsections:

- Accounts reached according to weekley day.

- Impression
- Account activity
- Top Posts
- Top Stories
- Top IGTV Videos

The "**Account reach**" section makes public the influence of your Instagram page and how people have interacted with it. This subsection displays the performance and influence of your Instagram account.

For example, from 17th sep to 23rd sep, the unique accounts reached by this Account are 409. You can see an increase of +122.2% of the Account reched in 1 week. This is a very good result.

Here's you can find two key metrics: Reach and Impressions.

Account Reach – The total number of unique Instagram users that have seen any of your posts in the past seven days.

Impressions – The total number of times that all your posts have been seen in the past seven days.

Remember that the Impression number must be higher than the Reach number because one person could see twice your video or post. So just to give you an idea.

Take the example of 5 people that use Instagram. All of them saw your post twice in 1 week. That means that your post's reach is 5, and the impressions = 5 (person) x 2 (twice) = 10 times.

Let's make another example :

Reach: 24 799 users

Impressions: 114 016 times

That is mean that each Instagram user has seen our posts 4.59 times = 114 016 total times/24 799 people.

Now you know better how to set up your metrics.

Interactions section of Activity Insights:

In this subsection, you can find the total number of actions taken on your Account in the past seven days. You can see these metrics per day as well, thanks to the chart that Instagram provides. Using the chart, you can find which day of the week has the highest Engagement. Note that, unfortunately, this section of Instagram Insights is limited only to the past seven days.

Accounts Reached

409 accounts

+122.2% vs Sep 17 - Sep 23

Thu   Fri   Sat   Sun   Mon   Tue   Wed

Accounts reached from Sep 24 - Sep 30

Impressions +45.9% vs Sep 17 - Sep 23	**1,640**
Account Activity	**96**
Profile Visits +52.3% vs Sep 17 - Sep 23	96
Email Button Taps 0% vs Sep 17 - Sep 23	0
Call Button Taps 0% vs Sep 17 - Sep 23	0

Here's what "Account Activity" insights mean:

Profile Visits – the total number of users that have visited your Instagram profile in the past seven days.

Email Button Taps – the total number of times users have tapped on Email on your BIO profile in the past seven days.

Call Button Taps– the number of times users have tapped on Call on your Bio profile in the past seven days.

Tracking these metrics is highly important to know whether your efforts to promote your Instagram account are successful, and should be a crucial part of any social strategy.
Regarding the three sub – sections: **Top Posts, Top Stories, and Top IGTV Videos**. I will illustrate them in the next chapter, **Content Interactions.**

Chapter 3: Content Interactions analytics

The **Content** section will help you find data relating to individual posts or stories on your Instagram profile.

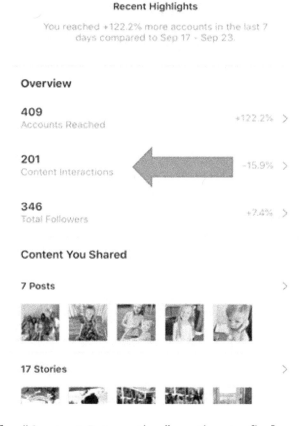

Tap on the "Content Interaction" section to find more details. The Content tab is splited into the following main subsections:

Posts Interactions;

Stories Interactions;

IGTV Interactions;

Top posts

Top Stories

Top IGTV videos

The content Intercation section illustrates the total number of interactions collect from posts, IGTV, and stories contents in the seven days. Instagram includes in the Interaction category the following actions: likes. comments, saves, and shares. Note that these four actions are the most important for the Instagram algorithm.

Top Posts section

In this section, you'll find all the essential Instagram insights of your feed's content from the past two years or from when you switched to a business profile.

In this section, you can find the feed ordered by the number of times your followers saw the current week's posts.

Note you can organize your data by **type, time, and type of interaction**.

To find the data above, you must follow the steps:

Step 1: Tap the hamburger icon in the top-right corner of your Profile.

Step 2: Tap the gear icon for "Insights."

Step 3: Next, hit "Content Interaction."

Step 4: Scroll **to the Top Post section** and Tap **"See All."**

Step 5: You will see the following screenshot.

These are the Instagram insights you can filter by Any, Impressions, one year, or 2 years; reach

I'll start with the **FIRST SUBSECTION of Posts** named "**Any**." Here you can select the post type that you want to track:
- Simple Photos;
- Videos;
- Carousel posts (more than one content) can add up to 10 images and/or videos in one large post.
- Shopping posts – a post that contains a shopping tag.

The SECOND SUBSECTION is named "Reach". You can find the following information:

Call Button Taps – The number of unique accounts that use your mobile phone contact to "Call" you, maybe they followed "Call to Action" set up by you.

Comments – You can find the total number of comments on each of your posts.

Email Button Tap – The number of unique accounts that followed the Call to Action to send you an email, using the Email indicated in your BIO.

Follows – The number of users that started following you because of your post.

Get Directions – The number of users who tapped Get Directions because of your post. To get this data you must add a location tag to your picture.

Impressions – The total **number of times** your post has been seen in general.

Likes – The total number of likes on your posts.

Profile Visits – The number of times your IG account was viewed.

Reach – The number of **unique accounts** that have seen your posts.

Saved – The number of unique users that saved your post.

Shares – The number of unique accounts that have shared your post.

Texts – The number of accounts sent you direct messaging (DM) because of your post.

Website Clicks – The number of times your website indicated in your BIO was clicked because of your post.

You can organize and order all your posts based on these Instagram insights to see which posts performed the best and worst.
You can also go deeper into each post to get more data. You can use the following method as well:

Step 1: Click on each post, then
Step 2: Tap '**View Insights**' will open the in-depth analytics.

You can see the image below for further information:

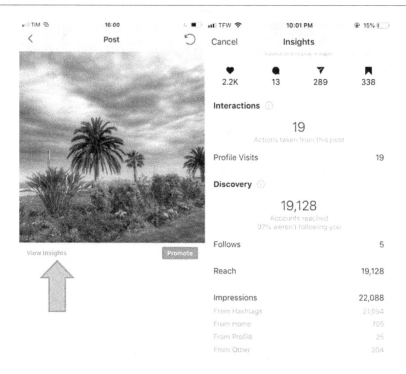

Under this section, you can see:
- The total interactions as profile visits (action is taken from this post).
- The breakdown of the Engagement (likes, comments, tag or save);
- The breakdown of the discovery of your post. This includes where all your impressions came from hashtags, directly through your Profile, home feed, or other options.

You can check the image example above to get more details.

For example, the picture offers the following information:
- Impressions – this post was viewed 22 0088 times by Instagram followers.
- Reach or Discovery – this post reached 19 128 unique Instagram users.

I would like to focus the attention on these two very important metrics: Impression and Reach.

Reach means that the post reached 19 128 unique people. Impressions refer that 22 088 times the post has been displayed on a mobile screen.
Pay attention to how many people save and share each post. Check how many followers you get from every post as well.

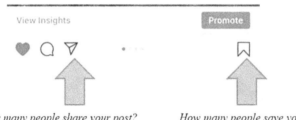

How many people share your post?   *How many people save your post?*

Retake my example. You can see that the post was saved 338 times and shared 289 times.
The Post subsection is the fastest way to check what type of content is performing best with your Audience, and also track how your engagement rate varies over time!
In the Discovery section of "View Insights", you can find if your hashtag strategy positively impacts reach and impression metrics. You can find more details on how to track hashtag performance in chapter 7.

The <u>THIRD SUBSECTION</u> of Posts is "Time Period".
Here you can find different options: 7 days, 30 days, 3 months, 6 months, 1 year, or 2 years.

Top Stories Section :

Stories are another subsection under the Content tab where you can find the Instagram insights of your Instagram Stories. These data can help you to understand how users view and interact with your Stories.

All these metrics allow you to shape and plan Story content for the future.

Under the "Stories" category you can find two subcategories: **Interaction** and **Time Period**.

To find these two subsections you need to follow the steps below:

Step 1: Tap the hamburger icon in the top-right corner of your Profile.

Step 2: Tap the gear icon for "Insights".

Step 3: Next, hit "Content Interactions".

Step 4: Scroll to "Top Stories" and tap "**See all**".

Step 5: You will see the following screenshot.

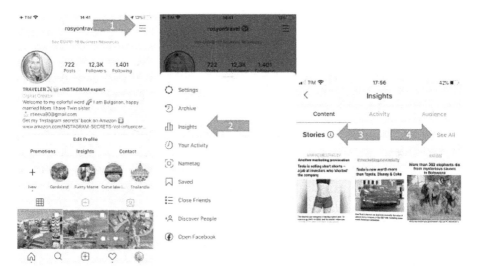

Select Time Period:

Here you can view Insights of your stories by 24 hours, 7 days, or 14 days. Remember that 14 days is the maximum time limit.

The Instagram Stories Interaction Insights include some categories similar to the Post section. I would like to focus your attention only on the metrics that are different as:

Back – the number of users that went back from this story. Back clicks would indicate the previous Story was highly relevant to your Audience as they re-watched it more than one time.

Exited – the number of times a user swipe from a story.

Forward - The number of users that skipped this Story post. If you have a large proportion of forwarding clicks, you could derive the Story wasn't captivating enough.

Link Clicks – in case you have more than 10 k followers. You can check how many users make swipe up and click on the links.

Next Story – the number of taps to see the next story. If the number of users that tap Next Story is high, it could imply your Story went on too long or became repetitive.

Impressions – The number of times your Instagram Story has been seen.

Reach – The number of unique accounts that viewed the post on your Instagram Story

Replies – The number of replies to a particular photo or video in your story. You are going to find these replies in your DM (direct messaging).

You have to scroll through the different options to check all parameters.
Using Insights tools for Instagram Stories could help you derive conclusions on the type of content that works best. The Insights will help you understand if you are creating the right content for your Instagram target audience and posting at the right time of day.

The Navigation section offers critical performance indicators such as Impressions, Reach, Forward, Back, and Next Story. You can understand better your Audience's interest thanks to these metrics.

You can also learn which Stories help boost the most follower interaction with the Replies insights. These are critical metrics and can improve your Instagram Story content according to your audience preferences.

Promotions Section of Content:

In the Content tab of Instagram Insights, you can track the metrics relating to any promotions and paid ads you've published or had running on your Profile. This section is available only if you run Promotion campigns.

You can view the following metrics:

The number of Profile Visits from your advertising posts.

The number of Reach, Impression, and Engagement on each post.

The Location, Gender, and Age of the Audience who viewed the post.

The last section is named Promotions and helps you to track the Insights for the posts that you've spent money on to boost the impressions and reach. In this section, you can view:

- **Impressions** – The total amount of times your post has been seen.

- **Reach** – The number of unique accounts that have seen your posts.

- **Audience demographics** – The age, gender, and location of the people who viewed your post.

- **Engagement** – The number of Saves, Likes, and Comments.

- **Profile visits** – The number of times your Profile was viewed.

Using these insights, you can evaluate your paid advertising campaigns, and view which feeds were most effective in reaching the business objectives you set.

These data will help you understand not only your target audience but will help determine if the content that you are producing is helping you achieve your goals.

Remember that it's important to frequently check your Insights and because Instagram only displays certain metrics from the past seven days.

I recommend that you track your stats once or twice per day.

Chapter 4: Total Followers analytics

The last Insight section is named "Total followers," and we can learn more about our **Audience**. This section will help you to get a better understanding of who your followers are and where they live. You can see how your follower number has varied from the previous week.

Hit the "Total Follower" section to open all sub- sections.
The first subsection is named "Growth"; you can find further information about your growing trend. You can track the total number of people that follow and unfollow your Account in the past 7 days. See the chart below.

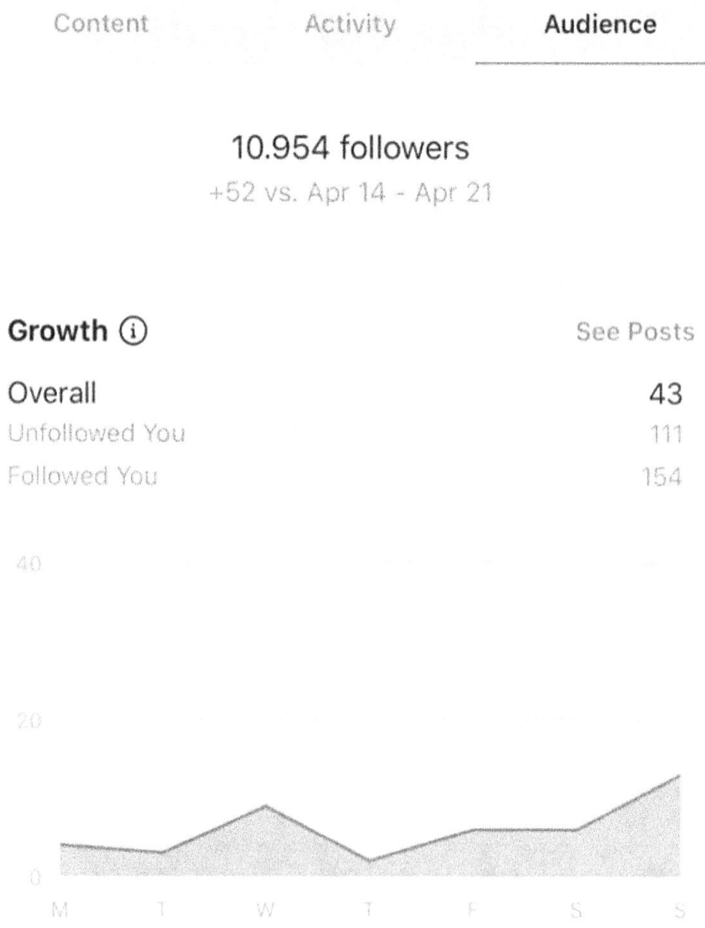

10.954 followers

+52 vs. Apr 14 - Apr 21

Growth ⓘ   See Posts

Overall   43
Unfollowed You   111
Followed You   154

40

20

0

M   T   W   T   F   S   S

If you tap the chart above in the middle, you will see the
growth day by day.

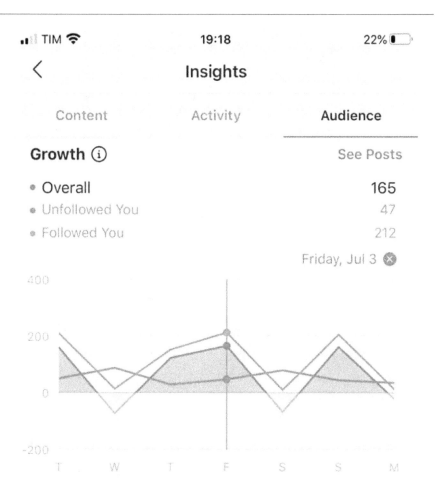

The **second subsection** is named "**Top Locations**."
The locations of your followers based on City and Countries.
Fundamental data that can help you to know the time zone of
your followers.

Within the Audience section of the Instagram Insights tool, you'll find three critical sets of information about your followers:

Age Range – The age brackets of your followers.

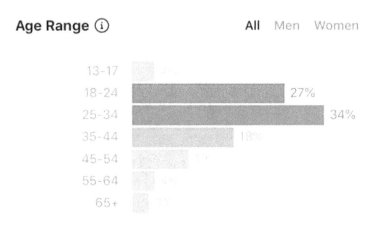

Gender – The percentage split of your followers: women and men.

Most active Times – The most active times of your followers, by the hour of the day and days of the week.

Content   Activity   **Audience**

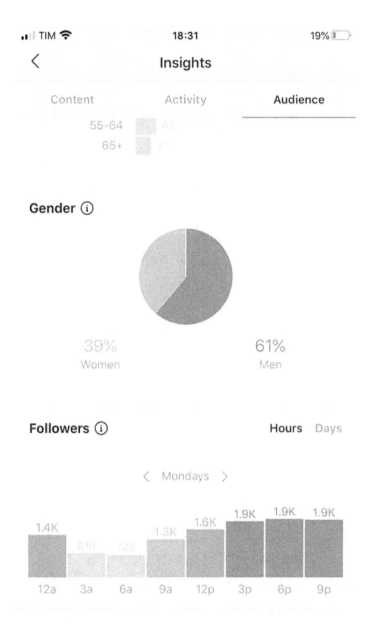

55-64

65+

Gender ⓘ

39%   61%
Women   Men

Followers ⓘ   **Hours**   Days

<   Mondays   >

1.4K   1.3K   1.6K   1.9K   1.9K   1.9K

12a   3a   6a   9a   12p   3p   6p   9p

The chart shows that the best hours to post on Monday is from 3 p.m. to 9 p.m. Thanks to this data you can also decipher the time in which your followers are most active, helping you better plan and schedule your Instagram posts to reach the possible people.

Instagram Insights is quite limited in how the analytics are presented – particularly for users needing report metrics to managers or clients.

So it's good to know that Instagram Insights can also be accessed using other services, including Hopper HQ; Iconosquare, Keyhole, Instagram Planning, and Scheduling Tool.

These tools help to see better all figures. So, if you need more detailed data, it's time to look at third-party apps or software.

Anyway, you can see, the Audience section reveals key Instagram insights about your followers, which can help build and improve your Instagram Strategy.

Chapter 5: How to analyze the performance of the hashtags on Instagram?

You need to track all the hashtags to be able to discover which ones bring in the most Engagement.

Tracking hashtags on Instagram is not complicated. You can find information regarding the performance of your hashtags right within the native app or using an ad hoc analytics tool.

With the "Insights" tool, Instagram added the ability to analyze how effective your hashtag strategy is in getting more views (or impressions) on your posts! Which is a great indicator of whether or not you've chosen the right hashtag - keywords for your strategy. Now you have a good reason to move to an Instagram business profile! Let me show you how to do this.

To access your Instagram data from the native app, simply select the post on which you want to check the "Insight figures", and follow these steps.

Step one: Open one of your posts.

Step two: Press the "View Insights".

Step three: Swipe up, and you'll get a full page of data for that post, including profile visits, follows, reach, and breakdown of how and where your post was discovered. Under the Impressions metric, you'll find 'From Hashtags' which tells you how many people found your Profile post through the hashtags you used.

Instagram provides aggregate data on hashtags, and you cannot track the performance of each hashtag. Instagram announces that at the end of 2020 all Instagram profiles are going to find hashtag breakdowns on the Insight page.

Today we can check only the aggregate hashtag metrics. See the example below.

Example:

Pay special attention to the "From Hashtags" metric located under "Impressions" data. This number tells you how many people discovered your post through the hashtags you used.

I recommend you after 3 h from the posting to check the hashtags that you used for the post, one by one. How you can do this.

Simply check each of them and check how is ranked your picture or video. If your feed is located in the first 12 pictures you can note down these hashtags as suitable for your Account and use them again.

Do not forget to use the " Related" option of hashtags that Instagram offers when you find the right hashtag for your Account. The related hashtags have to be tested as well. Think that the related hashtags that Instagram offers for one hashtag have good potential for your Account. Check the image below where to find the related hashtags.

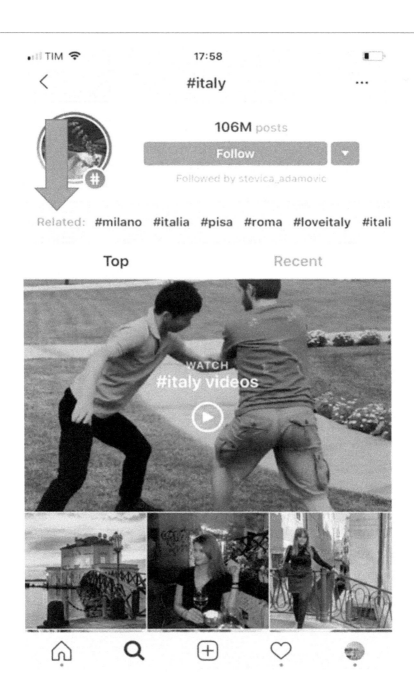

I would like to share with you the names of some analytics tools that I consider efficient:

Infosquare (https://pro.iconosquare.com),

Later (https://later.com/), and

Socialinsider (https://www.socialinsider.io/).

All applications mentioned offer a free trial. Try to use this free trial period to get all your analysis. Try to track the individual hashtag performances and see the impression metrics of each hashtag. When you track down the performance of each hashtag, you are in a position to make informed decisions on the next posts and how to improve your hashtags strategy.

You can find all the tips on how to use Hashtag for your strategy in my book: Instagram Secrets Vol 5: HOW to use Instagram HASHTAGS. Become an influencer and build a business with no money on Instagram.

Chapter 6: The 6 Instagram metrics that you must track

I would like to inform you that the most important factor for the Instagram algorithm is not possible to track. And this factor is named – Time. Time spent on posts or stories content is the most important metrics for Instagram.

Trivially, how long a person stays on your post. Think about a video. How many times do you concern it? Or think of a carousel. how long does it take you to read it all? And to read a nice long description? For this reason that sometimes you happen to have posts that maybe receive fewer interactions, even they don't go so badly from the point of view of coverage. It is not possible to get any information about these metrics, but we can focus on other metrics.

To feel more prepared to deal with the insight, you need to figure out which metrics data to focus on.

Here's the list of all the important Instagram metrics that you need and you can monitor through Instagram. Tracking and measuring means you can optimize and grow you're following authentically while having real results backing up your decisions for what to do next.

Let's dive into the analytics that you need to track mandatory through the Instagram platform. I would like to focus your attention on the following 3 categories:
- Generic metrics;
- Post metrics;
- Stories metrics;

GENERIC METRICS

In this category, I would like to include Follow growth, DM received, and website clicks per month.

"Follow growth" check just to check if your strategy is working. Do not be obsessed with these metrics, just check if you go in the right direction Do not forget that it is most important to have an engaged audience and not just to grow.

Make this analysis once per month.

Website clicks it is very important if you have a web site link in your bio. So you can track how many people visit your website thanks to your Instagram profile. It is better to check these figures weekly.

DM received, there is no automatic way to check the number of DM received you have to count them manually and to write down the number each week to check if you improve your Engagement.

POST METRICS

This category includes the following metrics:
- Saves
- Shares
- Comments
- Profile visits
- Follower's gain with the post.
- Hashtags used to try to find the posts with the best hashtags that you used.

Check Chapter 3: Content insights to get information on how to find all the metrics figures listed above. You have to focus your attention on Most commented, saved, and shared posts. Check the types of content that your target saving and sharing. Try to focus on creating this kind of content that the people share, save, or comment on.

After that check the post that generated the majority of profile visits and followers.

The hashtags mix that you used is very important as well. Hashtag's strategy is could improve your impression rate and reach rate.

Impressions refer to the total number of times your post saw.

Reach refer to the total number of unique Instagram users that have seen your post.

It also includes posts that didn't receive likes or comments. Looking at the Insights, you can analyze how well you're promoting your content on Instagram.

Using hashtags ensures your content reaches a wide audience, improving your impression and reach score. Pay close attention to each of your posts to know which trends help promote your content to your target audience.

I can say that is a good result if your posts reached more than 40% - 50% of accounts that weren't following you.

So it is really important to check on how your content performing and at least once a month you can tweak your content strategy and do more of what's working well.

Make this analysis once per month.

The engagement rate is not so important today as a shared and saved rate of one post, but I would like to explain to you what is it and how to calculate it.

Engagement Rate per post is the total number of people who saw a post and left a "Like" or "Comment" on it divided by your total number of Instagram followers.

To win on Instagram, you need to be regularly analyzing your results, and there's nothing better than tracking your engagement rate on Instagram.

How do I calculate my engagement rate on Instagram per post?

It's much easier than it looks. Say you have 2 500 followers, your Engagement is measured by your likes and comments combined per post, divided by your following.

Get a pen and paper and select a post to analyses. Note down the number of comments and numbers of likes that post received. Let's say your total likes were 137 and comments came to 10.

137 + 10 = 147

You then need to take this magical number and divide it by your total followers, and times it by 100 (this will give you the percentage).

147 / 2,500 x 100 = 5.88%

Your total engagement rate for this post is 5.88%, which is sitting smack bang in the middle of the average engagement rate on Instagram.

You can find a lot of online websites that could calculate the average engagement rate of your Profile for free. I would like to give you some name as an example: https://www.ninjalitics.com/

Ninjalitics web site gives you an excellent analysis of your Profile for free.

Here are the industry standard guidelines for engagement rates of an account:

<1,000 followers: 8%

between 1,000 and 5,000 followers: 5.7%

between 5,000 and 10,000 followers: 4%

between 10,000 and 100,000 followers: 2.4%

> 100,000 followers: 1.7%

Keep in mind; several things influence the engagement rate on Instagram, such as the time of each post, the frequency of posting, the number of followers, the content and the messaging, and the Instagram algorithm (and the limitations that sometimes come with it).

As your follower count increase, you may find that your reach rate decrease so be prepared.

STORIES METRICS

Regarding Stories metrics. The most important thing to track is the Retention rate.

The retention rate is the percentage of people that stay watching your story from the beginning to the end.

Check the first story of the day and the last story to get the retention rate. I would like to give you an example.

Let's say that your first story of the day has 104 views and your last story has 75 views This means that 28% percent of viewers drop off. That is means that the retention rate is 72%=75/104.

The formula for the retention rate is the following:

$$RR = (LSVC*100)/FSVC$$

Where

- RR is Retention Rate,
- LSVC is Last Story View Count, and
- FSVC is First Story View Count.

You could use this parameter to compare retention rates per day or you could even compare RR by content type, say, for example, comparing a stream of «behind the scenes» stories versus a stream of «lifestyle and outdoors» stories.

There is no standard number for rotation rate because everything depends on the niche, industry, picture that you have.

But basically, you can bench your previous progress. You always have to try to improve your retention rate.

I would like to share with you the marketing chart created by SocialInsider.

You can see that the average reach rate of the stories is higher for the small accounts and lower for the accounts with more than 100 k followers.

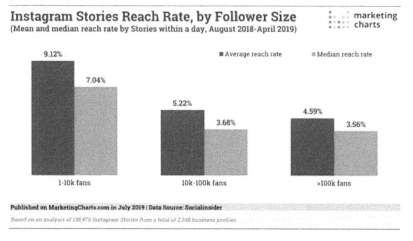

It is important to check, the numbers of replies and comments that you get for each story to understand how engaging is your content.

Make the analysis twice per month. Stories metrics are stored in analytics just for 14 days and that's why it is important to check them every 2 weeks.

Check these analytics every 2 weeks.

Chapter 7: How to use Instagram Insights for your social strategy

No matter where you are in your Instagram journey, Instagram Insights can help you find and reach success faster.

Use Instagram Insights to find the best time to post on Instagram

Understanding the best time to post on Instagram is even more critical now that you can schedule posts directly to Instagram.

Why does the time you post on Instagram matter?

Instagram's algorithm gives preference to posts with more Engagement. This means users see posts that are popular, not in chronological order the way they did in the past. However, Instagram does give a slight edge to recent posts, which is why you want to post when your Audience is online.

You can find all details about the Instagram algorithm in my book Instagram Secrets Vol 4 HOW to OUTSMART Instagram ALGORITHM. Become an influencer and build a business with no money on Instagram. (Short social media marketing book).

Use Instagram Insight to better understand your Audience

Who is your Audience? One of the most important questions to make. Instagram Insight can help you with the answer.

There, you can find out where most of your Audience is located, their age, gender, and more. You can also drill down to see age ranges specifically for men and women.

You can use this information to create content that better connects with your Audience. For more detailed demographic information, consider doing a poll using. The Poll feature in Instagram Stories is an important tool to gain more insights into your Audience's likes and dislikes.

One of the most important things is to find your Target audience and I can help you with my book: Instagram Secrets Vol 1: HOW to find the right Instagram AUDIENCE. Become an influencer and build a business with no money on Instagram. (Short social media marketing book).

Determine what type of posts do well

How do you know what types of posts your Audience likes? You could build a strategy based on what you think your Audience is into or you could look at the data and get solid stats that tell you what your Audience is actually into.

To see what type of content your Audience is interested in, navigate back to your Insights page, then click on the Content tab.

Here, you will see information about how many posts you have posted in the past week as well as feed posts showing which posts were viewed the most.

For example, you could see which posts got the most comments in the past 30 days and use that information to create a strategy for the next 30 days of content for your Account. Or, if you see that videos are doing well, you could plan to include more videos.

Clicking on each specific post will give you statistics about reach, likes, comments, messages, and profile visits.

Once you understand what types of content trigger specific actions, you can then use that information to help you reach your broader Instagram marketing goals. For example, if you know product photos trigger a significant increase in reach, you know to post product photos when you want more people to see your posts.

You can find a lot of tips on how to create killer content in my book: Instagram Secrets Vol 3: HOW to CREATE Instagram KILLER CONTENTS. Become an influencer and build a business with no money on Instagram. (Short social media marketing book).

Track your most successful Instagram Stories

Instagram Stories are a feature of Instagram similar to Snapchat. You can post images or short video clips that expire after 24 hours.

Many brands are using Instagram Stories to tease about upcoming launches, to connect with their Audience, or share behind the scenes information. A recent study found that 1 in 4 Gen Z and Millennial shoppers look for stories created by brands and products they are considering purchasing.

Brands that verify their accounts or have more than 10,000 followers can post links in stories, which makes stories more actionable and even shoppable.

Through Instagram Insights, you can view much of the same information about Stories that you can see about posts, including reach and impressions.

Remember that you can turn your best Instagram stories into Instagram Highlights and have them live on your Profile forever!

Track website clicks and profile visits

In addition to engagement metrics, Instagram also tracks website clicks and Profile visits. These metrics can be particularly important since Instagram gives most users just the one link — the bio link.

So, what is the purpose of tracking website clicks? For starters, it is a way to see if posts with captions like "Click the bio link to read more" actually work. Or, if you decide to use an Instagram link tool, like Linktr.ee, website clicks can show you if those tools are effective at driving more traffic.

Here you can see how many actions were taken by users on your Account, including website clicks and profile visits. You can also see what days most actions are taken, which allows you to plan your posts on days with more Engagement.

Chapter 7: Facebook creator Studio

You've Probably Never Heard about Facebook Creator studio. In 2019 Facebook's Creator Studio incorporated the Instagram dashboard.

You can find Facebook Creator Studio at the following link: https://business.facebook.com/creatorstudio/.

Instagram Creator Studio is ready to help you manage all of your Instagram feeds, get insights data from desktop, monetize your content, and more!

What are the advantages of Instagram users? Facebook Creator offers the opportunity to use one device and dashboard to get deeper insights into your data for both Instagram and Facebook.

The new integration between Instagram and Facebook Creator Studio will allow you to view your Instagram activities on your computer desktop.

The biggest advantages are that you can have a one-stop-shop for reporting on Instagram and Facebook platforms.

Comparing your data is simple because you can just tap the Facebook Icon to see your stats data and then tap the Instagram icon and compare your data in real-time.

How do I access Creator Studio on Facebook?

To find the Creator studio instrument, log into your Facebook Page, go to "Publishing Tools" and under "Tools" click on "Creator Studio" or visit the following link: https://business.facebook.com/creatorstudio/

Previously, the Creator Studio tool was only available for Facebook Pages and now you can use it for your Instagram account as well.

With the new Instagram Creator Studio, Instagram users get access to a lot of new tools and features, including the ability to schedule posts, videos, and IGTV videos!

Here's everything you need to know about Instagram's new Creator Studio:

You can find below two illustrations taken from the Instagram guide on how to use the Facebook creator tool.

I would like to share with you how the Insight section is displayed in the Creator Studio tool.

INSIGHTS: ACTIVITY

Refine your content strategy through activity insights

Interactions

View the number of actions your audience has taken on your account in the last 7 days, including profile visits, plus the number of click throughs to your website, email, and more!

Discovery

Accounts Reached:

The number of unique accounts that have seen your posts over the last 7 days

Impressions:

The total estimated number of times all of your posts have been seen compared to the previous 7 days

Tip! Hover over charts to view daily metrics!

Do not forget to check the Audience subsection as well.

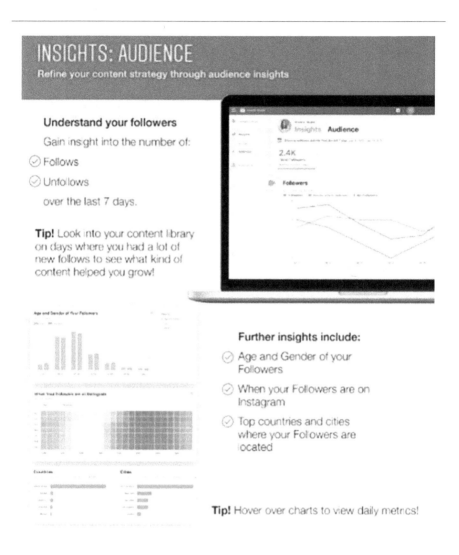

INSIGHTS: AUDIENCE
Refine your content strategy through audience insights

Understand your followers

Gain insight into the number of:

✓ Follows

✓ Unfollows

over the last 7 days.

Tip! Look into your content library on days where you had a lot of new follows to see what kind of content helped you grow!

Insights   Audience

2.4K

Followers

Further insights include:

✓ Age and Gender of your Followers

✓ When your Followers are on Instagram

✓ Top countries and cities where your Followers are located

Tip! Hover over charts to view daily metrics!

According to me the Audience chart that shows when your followers are on Instagram is organized better than the mobile app.

For further information on how to use the Facebook Creator tool for your Instagram account consult my book: **Instagram Secrets Vol 11:** HOW to use Instagram AUTOMATION TOOLS. Become an influencer and build a business with no money on Instagram.

Chapter 8: The homework section

The first thing to do is to take a paper and pen or to open one file in Excel.
I would like to ask you to start to fill in the following tables:

GENERIC METRICS

You have the following three tables:

- How many new followers do you get per month: month/number of followers?

-

month growth followers	growth per month
jan	120
feb	100
march...	

- How many DM do you receive per month: month/number of DM?

-

month DM	number of DM
jan	10
feb	20
march	30

-

- How many web site clicks do you get: month/number of clicks?

website clicks	clicks per month
check the website clicks weekly	
jan	10
feb...	20

POST PARAMETERS

saves in 1 week	how many saves		shares in 1 week	how many saves		coments in 1 week	
post 1	4		post 1	2		post 1	2
post 2	10		post 2	4		post 2	4
post 3	23		post3	5		post3	5
check the content which gets more saves			check the type of content with biggest number of shares			check the type of content with biggest number of coments	

You have to check:
- **How many saves do you get in 1 week and each month?**
- Post 1 - number of saves
- Post 2 – number of saves
- Post 3 – number of saves....

- **How many shares do you get in 1 week and each month?**
- Post 1 –numbers of saves
- Post 2 – numbers of saves
- Post 3 – numbers of saves......

- How many comments do you get in 1 week and each month?
- Post 1 – numbers of comments
- Post 2 – numbers of comments
- Post 3 numbers of commenst .....

STORIES PARAMETERS

STORIES METRICS	
Calculate the Retention rate of each day of the month	RR = (LSVC*100)/FSVC
day 1 of Jan	Where; RR is Retention Rate ; LSVC is Last Story View Count; - FSVC is First Story View Count
day 2 of Jan	

You have to check:
- Calculate the day retention rate.

$$RR = (LSVC*100)/FSVC$$

Where:
- RR is Retention Rate,
- LSVC is Last Story View Count, and

FSVC is First Story View Count

These tables can help you to make the first fast analysis of your Account. So try to use them.

Now we can have another 2 exercises. I have prepared two charts for you and I would like to ask you to answer what the numbers indicate?

Chart A:

1) ....
2) ....
3) ....
4) ....
5) ....

Chart B

Chart B)

1) ....
2) ....

3) ....

4) ....

5) ....

Answers:

Chart A

1) The post gets 62 likes.

2) The post gets 84 comments.

3) The post was shared with 4 Instagram users.

4) The post was saved 8 times.

5) The post generated 62 visits to Instagram, BIO, and Profile.

Chart B

1) The post generates 9 clicks on the website indicated in the BIO section of the Account.

2) The post reached 3 982 unique Instagram users, 76% of these accounts did not follow the Profile.

3) The post generates 12 follows.

4) The post was viewed 4 308 times, which means that on average 1.08 times =4308/3982.

5) 2768 impressions from 4308 total impressions were generated from Hashtags. So the Hashtag strategy was excellent because the post was viewed from 76% of accounts that didn't follow the Profile.

6) 898 impressions from 4308 total impressions were generated from the home page. That is means that the post was displayed on the feed page of the followers of the Account.

7) 26 impressions from 4308 total impressions were generated from the direct profile visit, which means that some Instagram users look for the Profile directly.

Conclusions

Congratulation that you finish "**HOW to use Instagram METRICS**', one of the 12 books of my Serial collection: Instagram Secrets.

As you know now Instagram Insights is a free tool for analyzing your content without ever leaving the app. The data you find helps you learn more about your Audience, what content is engaging them, and how your ads are performing. Use this valuable information to guide the type of content you create for your Audience and when you publish it.

Insights data helps business owners and marketers better understand how to be successful on the photo-sharing platform based on their specific Audience.

Instagram metrics can help you better understand your customers. What do they like? When do they spend most of their time online? How can you better reach them? These are critical questions you need the answers to when you're trying to market your product or service.

The more data and answers you have, the more tailored you can be in your marketing approach, and the more likely you are to share content that engages with your followers and compels them to convert.

I would like to show you the chart prepare by Later about what are some of the factors that impact who you consider being an influencer.

The first most important factor is the Engagement and now you know where to find the right metrics to evaluate your engagement rate.

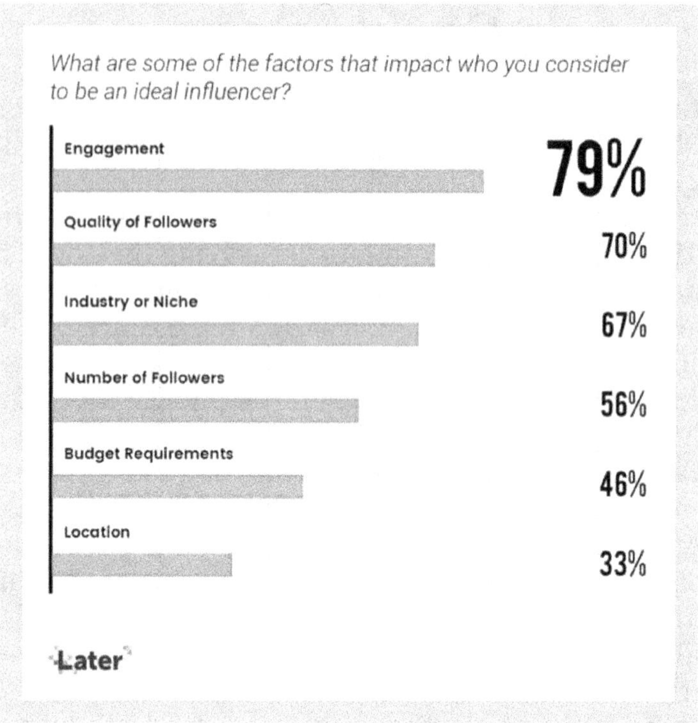

What are some of the factors that impact who you consider to be an ideal influencer?

Engagement
79%

Quality of Followers
70%

Industry or Niche
67%

Number of Followers
56%

Budget Requirements
46%

Location
33%

Later

Social media will always continue to evolve which means that each social media platform will have to keep innovating. That means that the Insights functionality of Instagram will inevitably evolve. So stay tuned to my Instagram page to get more news and updates:@rosyontravel.

When you create your Instagram content think always about the **3C Rule: Coherence, Constancy, and Competition**.

Other books

I hope that this book added value and quality to your social knowledge. If you enjoyed this book and found some benefit in reading this, I'd like to inform you that you can find in the Kindle store (Amazon) the following short guides that make part of the serial set.

Instagram Secrets Vol 1: HOW to find the right Instagram AUDIENCE. Become an influencer and build a business with no money on Instagram. (Short social media marketing book).

Instagram Secrets Vol 2: HOW to Build the Perfect Instagram Profile. Become an influencer and build a business with no money on Instagram. (Short social media marketing book).

Instagram Secrets Vol 3: HOW to CREATE Instagram KILLER CONTENTS. Become an influencer and build a business with no money on Instagram. (Short social media marketing book).

Instagram Secrets Vol 4 HOW to OUTSMART Instagram ALGORITHM. Become an influencer and build a business with no money on Instagram. (Short social media marketing book).

Instagram Secrets Vol 5: HOW to use Instagram HASHTAGS. Become an influencer and build a business with no money on Instagram. (Short social media marketing book).

Instagram Secrets Vol 6: HOW to use Instagram METRICS. Become an influencer and build a business with no money. (Short social media marketing book).

Instagram Secrets Vol 7: HOW to use Instagram DIRECT Messaging, Become an influencer, and build a business with no money on Instagram. (Short social media marketing book).

Instagram Secrets Vol 8: HOW to use Instagram IGTV content. Become an influencer and build a business with no money on Instagram. (Short social media marketing book).

Instagram Secrets Vol 9: HOW to use Instagram CONTESTS. Become an influencer and build a business with no money on Instagram. (Short social media marketing book).

Instagram Secrets Vol 10: HOW to use Instagram INFLUENCERS. Become an influencer and build a business with no money on Instagram. (Short social media marketing book).

Instagram Secrets Vol 11: HOW to use Instagram AUTOMATION TOOLS. Become an influencer and build a business with no money on Instagram. (Short social media marketing book)

Instagram Secrets Vol 12: How to generate PROFITS from Instagram. Become an influencer and build a business with no money on Instagram. (Short social media marketing book).

Do not forget about my special Bonus. Get one of my books for free. Send me an email at rtineva80@gmail.com. Please indicate the name of the book that you bought and the day. Send the name of the new book as well.

About the author

Hello, nice to meet you in this virtual space. Now it's time to introduce myself.

My name is Rosy Toneva, and I am a Commercial and Marketing B2B expert for some of the largest European Airlines. I enjoy traveling, writing, snapping pictures. I spend time daily writing and updating my Instagram blog @rosyontravel. I believe in one religion - Traveling!

I love educating and inspiring other people to succeed and live the life of their dream. I often repeat myself: If more than 50% of my brain believes it, it will come true.

I think that social media allows people to interact with others and offer multiple ways for marketers to reach and engage with consumers.

Now I would like to share with you how I started this project.

In April 2019, I decided to test my Instagram profile. I wanted to grow my Instagram account through my two passions, "Travel and Marketing". At the time, my account @rosyontravel had around 560 followers. I wanted to increase my followers in an organic way (no buying fake followers), no huge investing. I just desired to see what I could do by putting forth a conscious effort as a normal person did. It's been an intense four-month experiment of seeing what works and what doesn't. After only four months, I gained 10k loyal followers.

Thanks to a lot of tests I prepared a set of twelve books, named Instagram secrets that you can find on Amazon. The advantage of these books is that they are very simple and do not offer trivial tips. The good new is that I am a normal person like you so you can just check my page and say hello.

You can follow my Instagram profile (@rosyontravel) to get further information and updated news about Instagram.

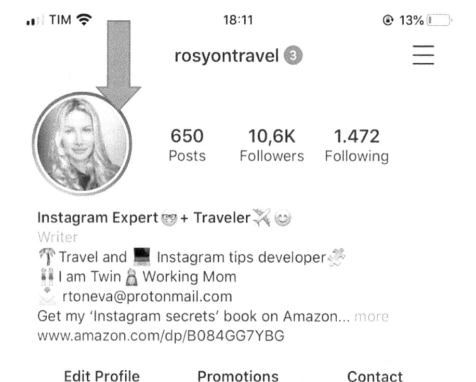

If you want to know more about Instagram secrets methods described in this book, please contact me personally. Send an email to rtineva8o@gmail.com or use Instagram Direct messaging.

One last thing

If you enjoyed this book and found some benefit in reading this, I'd like to hear from you and hope that you could take some time to post a review on Amazon. Your feedback and support will help me to greatly improve my writing craft for future projects and make this book even better.

I wish you all the best in your future success.

Common Instagram terms you should know

Bio - This is the biography of your Profile on Instagram. This is your place to tell the world a little bit about yourself. You can use text, emojis, hashtags, and even '@' mention profiles here.

Mention - This is how you get someone's attention on Instagram. Begin with the @ symbol, followed by their handle or name. If you're following them, you'll find their handle in the first couple of autocomplete options. You can mention someone in a variety of places on Instagram, including in your bio, comments, or even in Instagram Stories.

Tag - Tag is different from Mention. You can only tag a person on a picture or a video. When you tag someone, it will show up in their Profile (in the tagged section next to their Gallery).

Instagram Algorithm – An algorithm is a detailed step-by-step instruction set or formula for solving a problem or completing a task. In computing, programmers write algorithms that instruct the computer how to perform a task. Instagram Algorithm is several rules that the application follows to protect her community from spamming users and to set up the company earning a strategy.

Instagram Bots – These are automated profiles masquerading as people. But sometimes, even legit profiles use automated bots (third-party services) to get your attention. If you come across random comments on your posts or a slew of likes seconds after you post a picture, a bot was probably involved in the process.

Business Profile - Instagram offers a simple way to switch from a personal profile to a business profile. You don't even need to be a registered business to use a business profile. And there are many advantages to converting to a business profile. You get access to action buttons in the bio and you get detailed insights from your followers. Plus, using a business profile is the only way to unlock features like embedding links in Stories and adding buy buttons to your posts.

Insights - Once you've converted to a Business Profile, you'll see an Insights button in the top toolbar in your Profile. Tap on it and you'll find a sea of useful information. You'll find out what the age and gender breakdown of your followers is, as well as the best time to post to Instagram for maximum Engagement.

Explore page - Tap on the Search button from the bottom toolbar and you'll end up in the Explore tab. This is the hodgepodge of everything that's trending on Instagram right now. On the top, you'll find topics, and below, a feed of popular photos and videos.

Home page - The Home screen is the list of activities of all the users you follow. Also referred to as the feed.

Swipe up –It is a feature that allows you to add links to your stories. Now, all Instagram business accounts with 10,000 or more followers can add links to Instagram Stories. Up until recently, this feature was only available to verified Instagram accounts (accounts with sign V).

IGTV - IGTV video is an app that can be used alone or in tandem with Instagram. It's essentially Instagram's answer to YouTube.

Instagram Stories - is a feature within the Instagram app where users can capture and post related images and video content in a slideshow format. In both apps, content is available for only 24 hours from the time of posting. Stories allow the addition of text, drawings, and emoticons to images or video clips.

Instagram contest - is a great way to get more followers, build an engaged audience, and grow your brand. The contest is a promotional scheme in which participants compete for prizes by accomplishing something that requires skill. Although no fee is charged for participating in a contest.

API – The term API is an acronym, and it stands for "Application Programming Interface." The API is not the database or even the server, it is the code that governs the access point(s) for the server. They allow us to go get data from outside sources. To explain this better, let us take a familiar example. Imagine you're sitting at a table in a restaurant with a menu of choices to order from. The kitchen is part of the "system" that will prepare your order. What is missing is the critical link to communicate your order to the kitchen and deliver your food back to your table. That's where the waiter or API comes in. The waiter is the messenger – or API – that takes your request or order and tells the kitchen – the system – what to do. Then the waiter delivers the response back to you; in this case, it is the food.

IP Address - It's a network address for your computer so the Internet knows where to send you emails, data, and pictures.
With this short guide, I'm going to give you a deep dive into how to use Instagram hashtags to increase your followers. Using the right hashtags is fundamental. If you include the right Instagram hashtags on your posts or stories, you will likely see higher Engagement than you would if you didn't have any.